TESTING AND ASSESSMENT IN THE NATIONAL CURRIC

Pupils between the ages of 7 and 11 (Years 3–6) cover Key Stage 2 of tl Curriculum. In May of their final year of Key Stage 2 (Year 6), all pupils take written National Tests (commonly known as SATs) in three core subjects: English, Maths and Science. Your child should already have taken some National Tests at the end of Key Stage 1 (Year 2) in Maths (number, shape and space), English Reading and English Writing.

At the end of Key Stage 1, children are awarded a National Curriculum level for each subject tested. When children eventually take Key Stage 2 tests, they are again awarded a level. On average, pupils are expected to advance one level for every two years they are at school. The target for pupils at the end of Key Stage 1 is Level 2. By the end of Key Stage 2, four years later, the target is Level 4. The table below shows the average target levels.

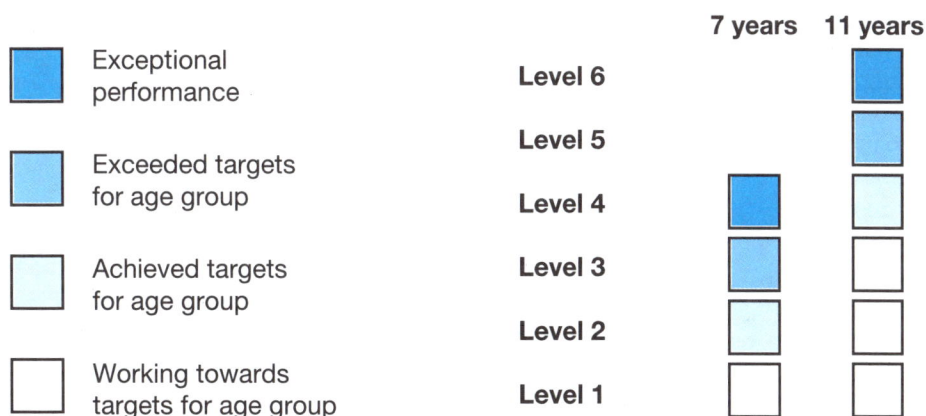

		7 years	11 years
◼ Exceptional performance	Level 6		◼
	Level 5		◼
◼ Exceeded targets for age group	Level 4	◼	◻
◻ Achieved targets for age group	Level 3	◼	◻
	Level 2	◻	◻
◻ Working towards targets for age group	Level 1	◻	◻

IMPROVING YOUR CHILD'S UNDERSTANDING AT KEY STAGE 2

This series will help you to work with your child to improve his or her knowledge and understanding of English, Maths and Science throughout Key Stage 2. There are four books for each subject – one for each year, starting with 7–8 year-olds. The activities in the books are appropriate to the target levels for each year and to the topics your child may study during that year.

These books may be used in conjunction with Letts' Progress Test books, also in the *At Home With The National Curriculum* range. The Progress books provide test materials to assess your child's level of knowledge at each year of Key Stage 2 and so tell you the areas in which he or she needs most help.

HOW TO USE THIS BOOK

The work in this book is mostly at Level 3 and is appropriate for the average 8–9 year-old. This book contains the following features:

Eleven four-page Units (pages 3–46) each incorporating:

- Notes to parents, explaining the relevance of the topic to the National Curriculum, a description of the activity and helpful 'Teaching points' advising you how to tackle common areas of difficulty.

- Two colourful information and activity pages for your child to work through with your help or on his or her own.

- Further questions and activities related to the topic, accompanied by more ideas for helping your child to understand the subject.

The topics covered in this book, and their page numbers, are as follows:

There is an Answers section at the back of the book.

Working through this book with your child

- Your child should not attempt to do all the activities in the book in one go. Work through each topic Unit together, allowing plenty of time for discussion and explanation of the subject. Encourage your child to attempt as many of the activities as possible without help, then use the further activities and ideas to expand on the subject. Do not move on to the next Unit until your child fully understands the one he or she is working on.

- Where children are asked to boil water or use sharp implements this warning symbol appears in the text: ⚠ ADULT HELP NEEDED

- The Answers section at the back of the book provides answers where possible. Check these with your child when each activity has been completed and discuss his or her findings. For some of the activities the answers depend on your child's results or predictions. You will have to judge the appropriateness of your child's answers.

- If your child has difficulty understanding a particular topic, the 'More ways to help your child' section offers methods of explaining a subject in less formal situations.

Equipment your child will need

The following may be needed for answering the questions in this book:

- a pen or pencil for writing, a pencil for drawing, a rubber and coloured pencils;
- a ruler;
- spare paper.

Individual topic Units might require additional simple equipment. Make sure you have everything your child needs before beginning each Unit.

Roots and leaves

Introduction:

Plants need water, light and warmth to help them grow. The roots of a plant take up water and anchor it in the ground. The leaves of a plant are its food factory – without light they go yellow. The green colour **chlorophyll** traps light, which is used with water and carbon dioxide to make sugar – the food a plant needs to grow.

National Curriculum:

Attainment Target 2: Life Processes and Living Things

At Key Stage 2 children should be taught that plant growth is affected by the availability of light and water and by temperature, and that:

*plants need light to produce food
and that water and nutrients are taken in through the root
and transported through the stem to other parts of the plant.*

At Level 3 children should be able to explain simply how the lack of light and water affects a plant's growth.

Activity:

In the first activity, children are asked to identify the best place for a plant to grow. Use three yoghurt pots of the same size (or small, clean flower pots). Make sure that the cotton wool is damp rather than soaking wet (as very wet cotton wool may rot the seeds and stop them from germinating). The second and third activities look at roots and how water taken up by the roots is lost through the leaves. When growing the onion, make sure that the water level is just below the bottom of the onion rather than touching it. You can drop charcoal into the bottom of the container to keep the water from smelling. Children could measure the roots or note how long it takes for the roots to get started. Plants are very sensitive to light, and in the fourth activity the potato shoot should soon start to grow. Use rubber bands to keep the box lid on.

The follow-up activities look at leaves. The covered grass should turn pale after a few days (light has been prevented from reaching the cells that make chlorophyll – the substance that makes plants green). Fixing a piece of paper or foil over the edge of a large leaf with a paper clip will give the same effect. In the last activity, there are fewer than ten basic designs for leaves so plants are sometimes classified according to their leaf-shape. Conifers have needle-shaped leaves, while broad-leaved trees may have simple leaves (each leaf grows in one piece at the end of its stalk) or compound leaves (several smaller leaflets joined to a single stalk, arranged along each side of the stalk or all attached to one point).

Teaching points:

Do not put seeds in direct sunlight as they can become scorched.

Make sure your child understands that plant growth depends on light, water and temperature. Plants make their own food in their leaves using sunlight. Roots anchor a plant and absorb water, while the Sun provides heat and light.

Roots and leaves

What does a plant need to grow?

1

Where will a plant grow best?

You will need:

three clean yoghurt pots
cotton wool
cress seeds
water

Fill the yoghurt pots with damp cotton wool.
Sprinkle cress seeds on top of each one.

Choose three different places to put the pots, for example a dark place,
a hot place and a very cold place.

Remember to keep the cotton wool damp.

What does each pot look like after two weeks? Draw in the seeds below.

Which one grew best? Do you know why?...

....

2

Plants take in water through their roots.

Fill a bottle with water and put an onion on top.
Leave the bottle somewhere warm and light.

What starts to happen after several days?

....

....

3

Water is carried from the roots, up the stem to the leaves.
Plants lose water through their leaves.

Here is a simple way to see this.

You will need:

a large, clear plastic bag
an elastic band or bag tie

Tie the plastic bag over the leaf of a tree as shown.
Leave it for a few days.

What has happened? Do you know why?

....

....

4

Plants will grow towards the light.
Here is a way to investigate this.

Make a potato maze

You will need:

a shoe box
cardboard
sticky tape
scissors
a sprouting potato

Cut a hole in the end of the shoe box and stick some flaps of card in as shown. Place the sprouting potato in the end furthest from the hole. Put the lid on. Stand the box somewhere light.

Check your potato every few days to see what happens.

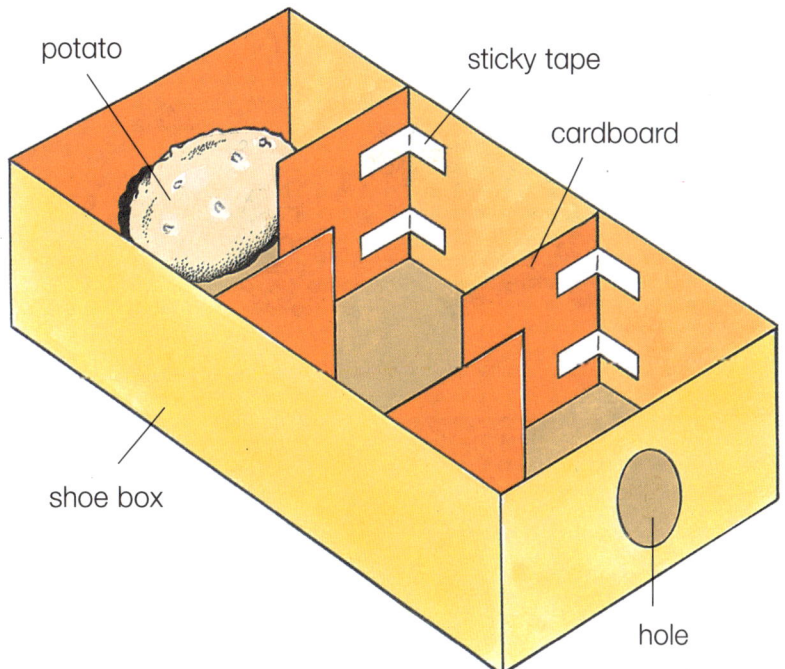

potato   sticky tape

cardboard

shoe box

hole

Now turn over ➤

Now try these ...

1 Cover some grass with a piece of black plastic
or wooden board. Leave it for several days.

What happens to the grass underneath? ....

....

Why do you think this happens? ....

....

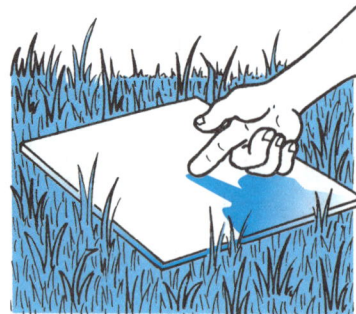

2 Collect leaves from as many different plants as you can find. Look
carefully at their shapes. Are they a single leaf or several small leaflets
joined together. Are they all one colour? Try and put the leaves into groups.

More ways to help your child:

Try growing seeds in different mediums, for example soil, sand and blotting paper.
Which are the most successful and why?

Grow bean sprouts: put some warm water and a handful of mung beans into a clear
jar, shake the jar for about a minute and drain off the water. Leave in a dark spot for a day.
Do the same thing the next day and for the following five days, when the bean sprouts
should be ready to eat.

Look at some different roots. For example, carrots and parsnips have swollen taproots
used for storing food, other plants such as grass have fibrous roots that spread out
over a wide area.

Shadows and reflections

Introduction:

Light travels in straight lines so it cannot go round obstacles in its path. When light hits a solid object, a shadow is formed. Light passes easily through transparent materials, but not through opaque materials. Materials that allow some light to pass through are called translucent. Most opaque objects have a rough surface which scatters light in all directions. Shiny materials, such as polished metal, have a smooth surface which reflects light in a regular way, producing a reflection. Flat shiny objects, such as mirrors, produce a sharp image.

National Curriculum:

Attainment Target 4: Physical Processes

At Key Stage 2 children are taught that:

light cannot pass through some materials leading to the formation of shadows and that light is reflected from surfaces.

At Level 3 children begin to make simple generalisations about physical phenomena such as which materials will form shadows. At Level 4 children should understand that light travels in straight lines and is reflected in a predictable way by mirrors and other shiny surfaces.

Activity:

In the first activity, children identify transparent, translucent and opaque materials. If your child is unsure what these words mean, demonstrate the differences with some of the materials suggested. The next activity looks at shadows and how they are formed. Before trying this activity, discuss with your child how shadows are formed (because light travels in straight lines it cannot bend round objects, so no light rays can reach the area behind the object, leaving it in darkness). You could use a simple diagram like this to help explain:

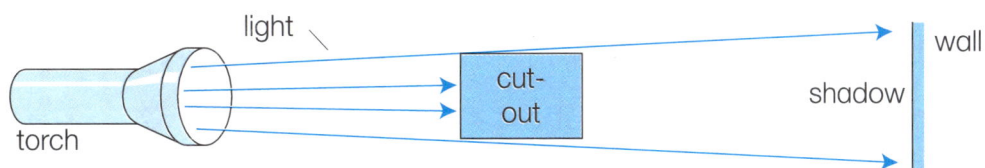

The third activity looks at which materials make good reflectors and the final activity looks at how shiny surfaces can produce different images. The back of a metal spoon is convex (which means it is curved outwards): light is reflected from a wide angle giving a wider view and producing a smaller image that is the correct way up. The front of a spoon is concave (which means it is curved inwards like a saucer): it produces a magnified image that is upside-down. See if you can find a range of other metal objects with curved surfaces for your child to look into and see the differences. The final task on the 'Now try these' page shows that light travels in straight lines. Your child will probably need assistance to set this activity up.

Teaching points:

Point out to your child that reflections in a mirror are reversed. This is simple to show with mirror writing where words appear back to front.

Shadows and reflections

Light can travel through some materials but not others.

1

Materials that let a lot of light pass through them are called **transparent**; materials that let some light pass through are called **translucent**; and materials that don't let any light through are called **opaque**. Look at these materials.

tissue paper   plastic   glass   thick curtain   silver foil

mirror   milk   oil   leather

Write a **T** if you think the material is transparent, an **L** if it is translucent and an **O** if it is opaque. Test your predictions with a torch.

2

When light cannot travel through an object a shadow is formed. Try making shadows on a wall with some cut-outs and a torch.

a What happens if you move the cut-out nearer the torch?

....

b What happens if you move the cut-out further away?

....

c Can you explain why this happens?

....

3

When you look in a mirror you see a **reflection** of yourself.
Light bounces off the shiny surface of the mirror back at you.
Lots of shiny surfaces reflect light. Tick the materials below
that you think would make good **reflectors**.

 ☐    ☐    ☐    ☐

silver   cardboard   bronze   steel

 ☐    ☐    ☐

water   polished wood   fabric

4

Find a metal spoon and give it a good polish.
Bring the spoon close to your eye.
If you look in the back of the spoon what can you see?
Turn it around. What can you see in the front of the
spoon?
Draw what you can see on the right.

The back of the spoon is **convex** or curved outwards.
The front of the spoon is **concave** or curved inwards.

How are the two images different?

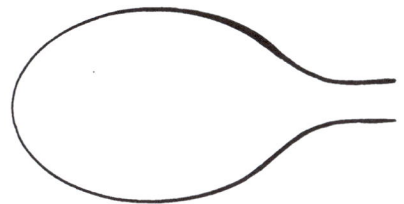

back

....

....

Which way up is your reflection?

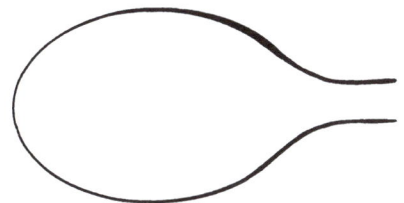

front

....

....

Now turn over ➤

9

Now try these ...

You can see that light travels in straight lines by making a **light beam**.

You will need:

card
scissors
a fork or a comb
a torch
a mirror

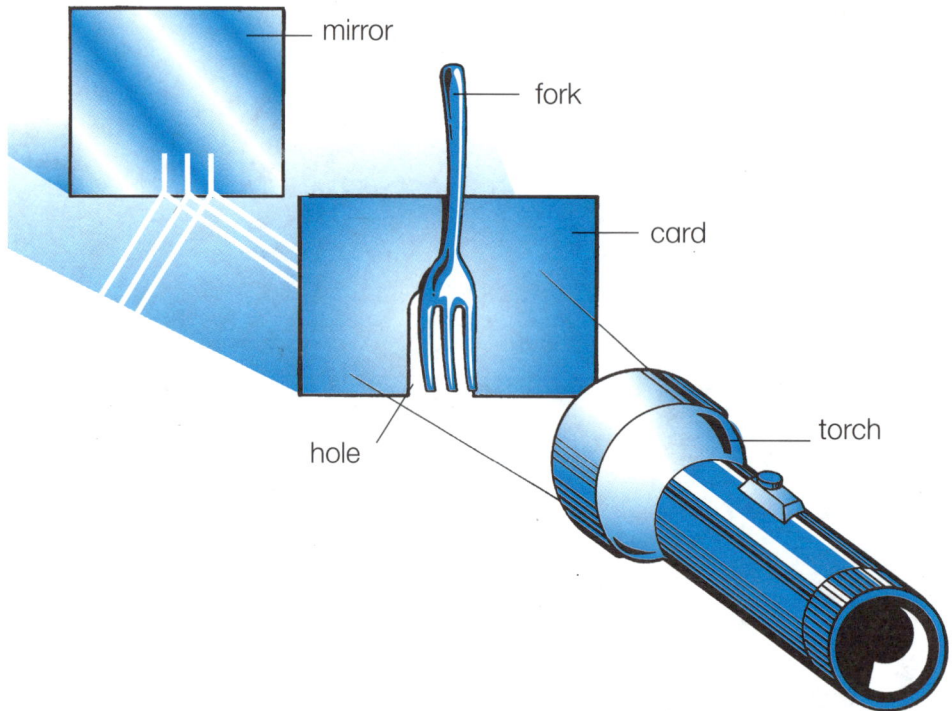

mirror

fork

card

torch

hole

In a piece of card, make a hole 3cm across.
Hold the fork or comb in front of the hole.
In a darkened room, shine a torch from behind the card through the fork.
Position the mirror so that it reflects the light.

What happens if you move the mirror?

....

Try out other objects instead of the mirror, such as silver foil.
What happens now?

....

....

More ways to help your child:

Discuss how mirrors can be useful, for example the rear view mirror in car, a periscope, checking under cars, looking inside your mouth.

Light gets dimmer the further you are from the source. Shine a torch on a wall and watch the pool of light get larger and dimmer as you move the torch further away.

Springs and elastic bands

Introduction:

Forces can change the shape of things. Springs are elastic. If you stretch them and let go, they spring back to their original shape and size. If you pull a spring too hard, however, it will lose this elastic quality and be unable to return to its original shape. If you press a spring downward, you compress it and it exerts a force on the object compressing it. Rubber behaves in a similar way when it is stretched or compressed.

National Curriculum:

Attainment Target 4: Physical Processes

At Key Stage 2 children are taught that:

> when springs and elastic bands are stretched they exert a force on whatever is stretching them; and that when springs are compressed they exert a force on whatever is compressing them.

At Level 3 children should use their knowledge to link cause and effect in the simple explanation of physical phenomena, such as the direction or speed of an object changing because of a force applied to it. At Level 4 children are expected to understand how motion is affected by forces.

Activity:

The first activity looks at springs and identifies some familiar uses for them. Children will probably be able to identify many more, for example inside ball point pens, spring-loaded gates and bathroom scales. Take the spring out of a ball point pen and look at how it works – how far can you stretch it before it looses its elasticity? The second activity asks children to draw what a spring would look like if it was compressed, or squashed. This goes on to look at what will happen when weights are added to kitchen scales. The fourth activity looks at how stretching an elastic band can be used to make a simple balance. Use known weights to mark off the scale behind the balance and make sure the balance hangs freely. Children should try out items of different size and weight, such as marbles, rubbers and pebbles, and record their weights using the scale. On the 'Now try these' page there are instructions for making a boat powered by an elastic band. Elastic bands and springs are good ways of storing energy for later use. Make sure there is a large enough gap at the back of the boat for the paddle to turn easily. Once children have made the boat, they might like to experiment with other designs for paddles and different shaped boats to improve their boat's performance.

Teaching points:

When looking at kitchen or bathroom scales, point out to your child that as the spring is compressed, or squashed, it moves the pointer round the scale to read off the weight.

Look for examples of springs and elastic bands being used, for example in clothes (elasticated waist bands, rubber soled shoes) or the buffers used on trains.

Springs and elastic bands

What makes a spring stretchy?

1 ──────────

Springs are made in a special way. If you push down on a spring, it will try and push back. Springs are made so that they are 'elastic'. This means they return to their normal shape after they are stretched or squashed.

Springs are used in beds. When a person lies on the bed the springs are **compressed**, or squashed.

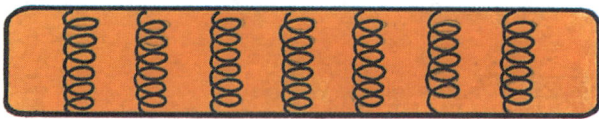 

Springs are also used in cars to give a smoother ride and in clocks and watches.

The spring inside a watch is wound up. It slowly unwinds to make the clock or watch tick.

Can you think of any other places where springs are used?

....

2 ──────────

Draw what this spring would look like if it was squashed.

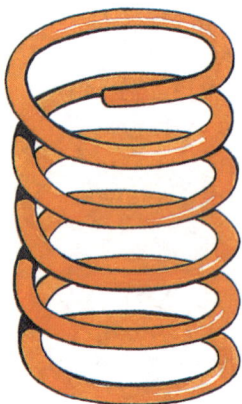

Springs like this are used in kitchen scales.

What happens when something heavy is put onto the scale?

....

3

Elastic bands are stretchy or 'elastic', too.

You can make your own spring balance with an elastic band.

You will need:

a clean yoghurt pot
a piece of string or
  strong thread
a drawing pin
a paper clip
a strong elastic band
some paper and a
  pencil

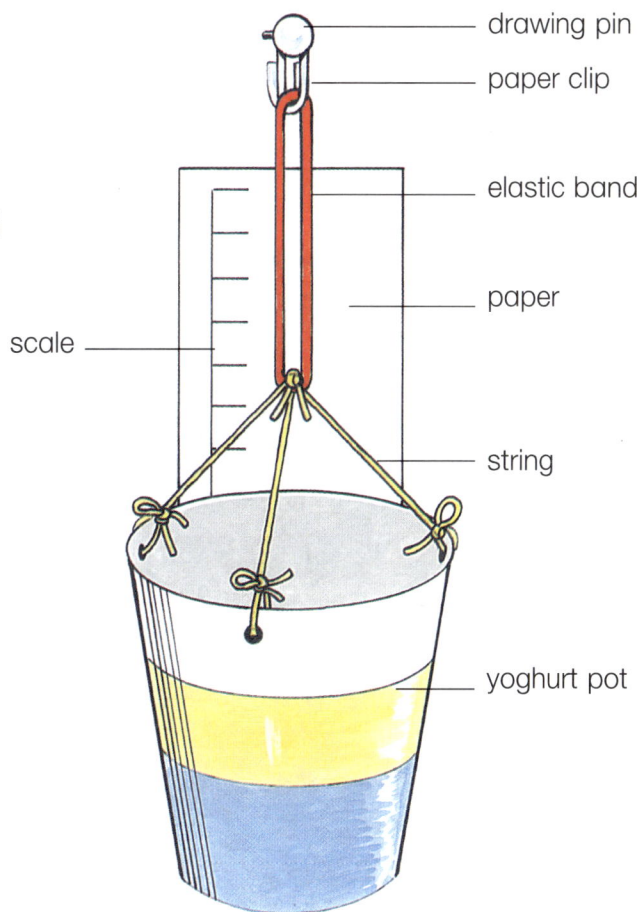

drawing pin

paper clip

elastic band

paper

scale

string

yoghurt pot

ADULT HELP
NEEDED

Hook up the yoghurt pot using a strong elastic band and some string as shown.

Draw a scale behind your balance. Do this by putting up a piece of paper behind your balance. Put different weights into the pot and mark where the top edge of the pot rests each time.

Use your scale to weigh different objects, such as marbles, pencils and toy cars. What happens to the elastic band?

....

Now turn over ➤

Now try these ...

A squashed spring stores energy. When you let go, the energy is released. Twisting an elastic band stores energy, too.

Make an elastic band boat

This boat has an elastic band for an engine.

You will need:

balsa wood
a strong elastic band
two drawing pins
a lolly stick

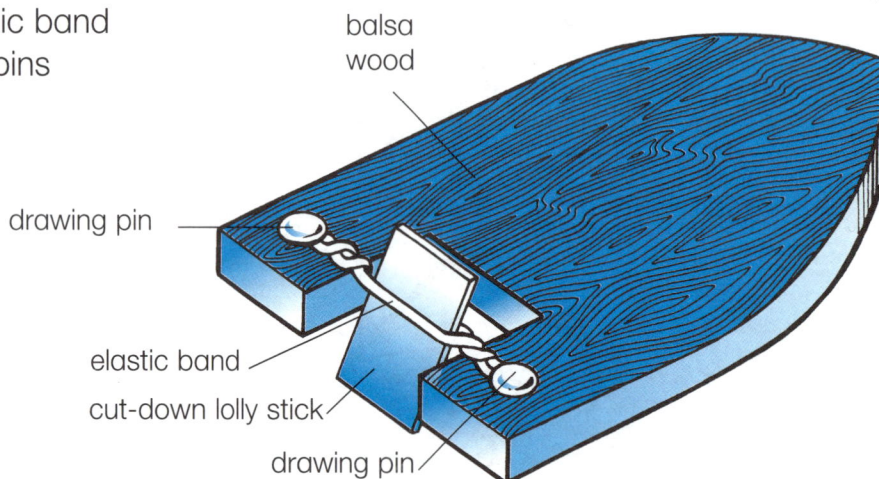

⚠️ ADULT HELP NEEDED

balsa wood

drawing pin

elastic band

cut-down lolly stick

drawing pin

Ask an adult to help cut out a boat shape from the balsa wood.
Push or bang in the two drawing pins as shown.
Fix the elastic band to the pins.
Ask an adult to cut the lolly stick to make the paddle.
Push the paddle between the elastic band.
Twist the elastic band as tight as you can using the paddle.
Put the boat into a bowl of water or a bath and let the paddle go.

What happens? ....

What happens if you wind the elastic band the other way?

....

More ways to help your child:

Supermarkets often have spring balances in the fresh produce section.

Modern electronic balances work in the same way as compression spring balances but are far more accurate.

Try finding other toys that work using springs (clock-work toys) or elastic bands (catapults).

Body talk

Introduction:

We need teeth to break up our food properly so that our bodies can digest it. There are three different types of teeth: incisors at the front of the mouth do the cutting; next to these are canines which tear food; and at the back are molars which chew food. Teeth are covered by enamel, the hardest substance in the body. Inside this is a layer of dentine. At the centre of a tooth is the pulp which contains blood vessels and nerves to send messages to the brain. Thin incisors have only one root to keep them embedded in the jawbone, while molars usually have three roots to help withstand the pressure of chewing food. Sugary foods attack the teeth which then start to decay. Certain foods such as milk and fish are good for the teeth because they contain calcium and vitamins needed for healthy teeth. During our lives we have two sets of teeth – milk teeth when we are children followed by a second set of permanent teeth.

National Curriculum:

Attainment Target 2: Life Processes and Living Things

At Key Stage 2 children are taught:

about the functions of the teeth and the importance of dental care.

At Level 3 children should appreciate the functions of different types of teeth and be able to give simple explanations about how diet and what we eat affects our health.

Activity:

The first activity looks at the position of different types of teeth and their function. Children could look inside their own mouths using a mirror to see if they can spot where the different teeth are located. Dental care is very important and the second activity could be emphasised by going over some simple rules, such as the importance of brushing your teeth on a regular basis. Encourage children to talk about why teeth need to be kept clean and why regular visits to the dentist are necessary. The third activity is a list of foods from which children have to choose those that are beneficial for teeth. Milk is a good source of calcium which helps teeth to grow strong and raw vegetables and crisp fruits such as carrots and apples help to keep teeth clean as you bite into them. The final activity on the spread looks at how sugary foods attack our teeth. Bacteria in the mouth break down the sugar in food to form acids which destroy the teeth. In the test, an egg whose shell is made of similar material to teeth, is left in a beaker of vinegar (a weak acid) to see what happens. The follow-up activities on the 'Now try these' page look at words connected with teeth and what is inside a tooth.

Teaching points:

Talk to your child about how teeth work and why they are an aid to digestion.

Ask your child to show you how to use a toothbrush – the best way to brush the teeth is by using small circles around each tooth rather than from side to side.

Body talk

Inside your mouth are teeth. You use them to bite and chew your food.

1

Teeth are different shapes to do different jobs.

Incisors are found at the front of the mouth.
These sharp teeth are used for cutting and slicing food.

incisor

Canines are longer and more pointed.
They are used for tearing and ripping food.

canine

Molars at the back of the mouth are large and flat.
They crush and grind up food.

Teeth are held firmly in the mouth by the gums.

molar

Can you name the different types of teeth in this diagram?

Fill in the spaces.

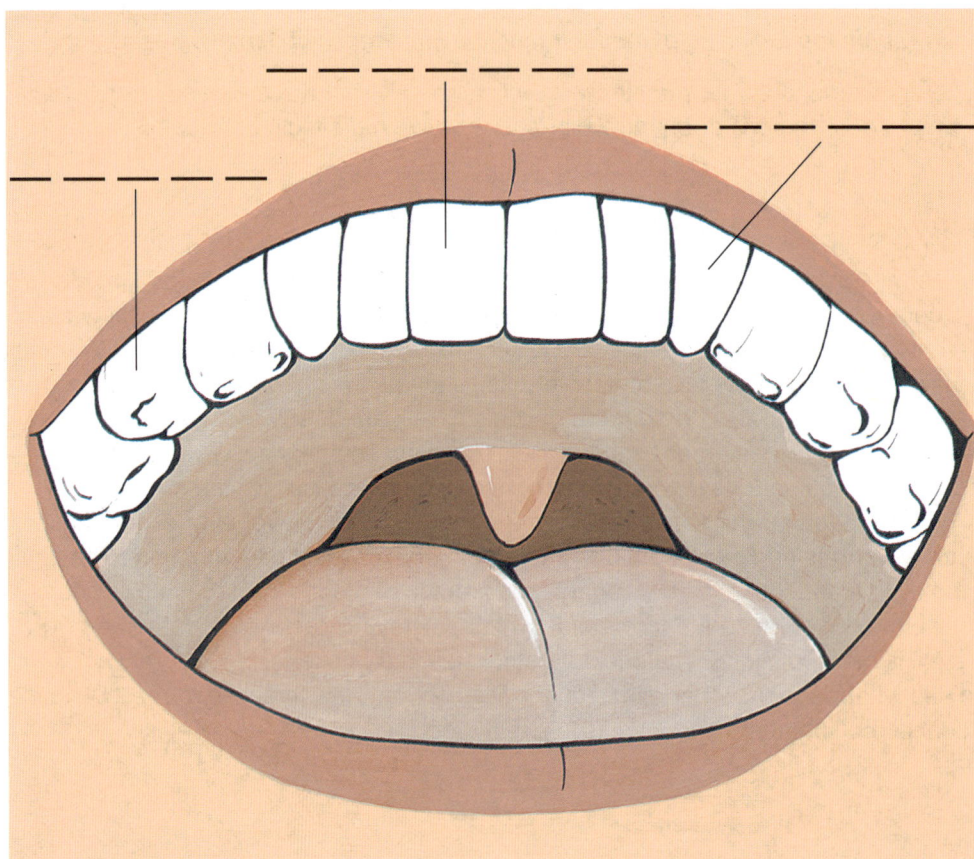

How many of each type of tooth have you got in your mouth?

....

2

It is important to look after your teeth and gums to keep them healthy. Write down three things you use to keep your teeth clean.

1 ....

2 ....

3 ....

When is the best time to clean your teeth?

....

3

Eating the right food is also a good way to look after your teeth.

Look at these foods. Circle those that are good for your teeth.

4

If you do not look after your teeth they will **decay**, or rot.

Try this test to see what sugar can do to your teeth.

You will need:

an egg
vinegar
a glass jar

Ask an adult to hard boil the egg. Pour the vinegar into the jar and put in the egg. Leave it for a few days. What happens to the shell?

....

....

This is what fizzy drinks can do to your teeth.

ADULT HELP
NEEDED

Now turn over ➤

17

Now try these ...

1 Unscramble these words to do with teeth.

CADEY ....   ISINCOR ....

NINACE ....   ROLMA ....

KILM ....   MUG ....

DENSITT ....   PASTTOTHOE ....

2 The outside of a tooth is covered by a hard layer called **enamel**.
This protects the **dentine** beneath. In the middle of a tooth is the
pulp which is full of nerves and blood vessels. The **root** holds the tooth
in place in the jawbone.

Look at this picture. It shows what is inside a tooth. Can you name the
parts? Use the words from the list below.

root   gum   bone   enamel   pulp   dentine

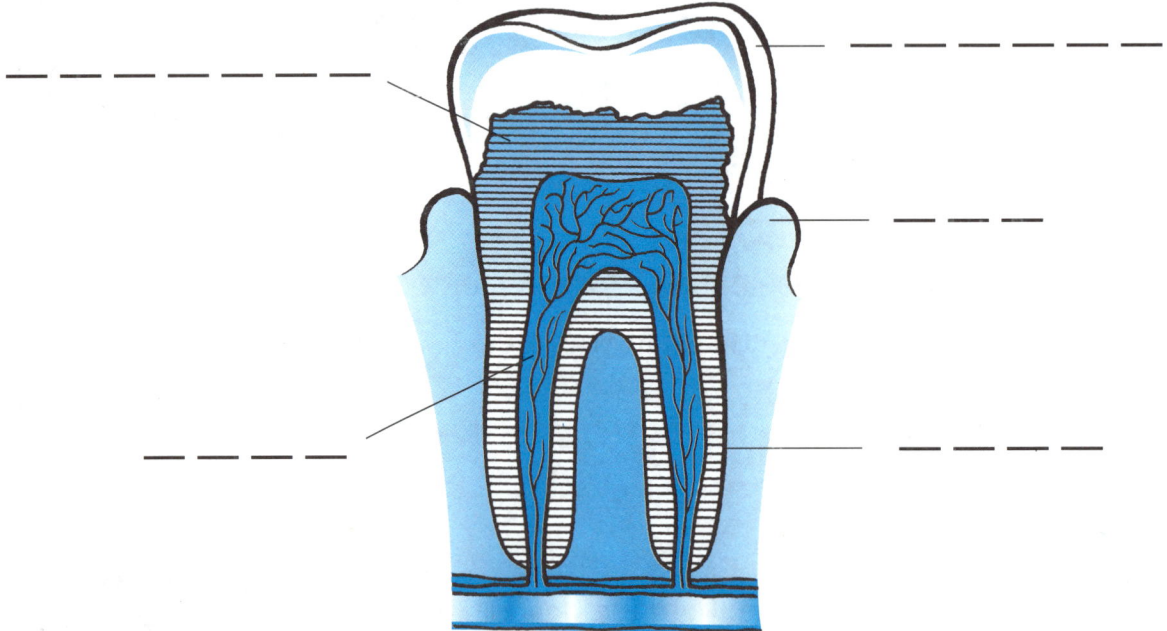

More ways to help your child:

Talk together about why regular visits to the dentist are a good idea and what happens
when you have a filling.

Discuss the teeth of different animals – lions have large canines for tearing prey, horses
and cows have very large molars to chew grass, and rodents have strong incisors to gnaw
away at hard nuts and seeds. Some animals' teeth are not for eating food – tusks are
huge front teeth used for frightening off enemies and sometimes for digging up food.

Friction

Introduction:

When two surfaces rub against each other they produce **friction** (the force that opposes sliding or slipping). The friction between our shoes and the ground stops our feet sliding when we walk forwards. Bicycles and cars use friction between their tyres and the surface of the road in a similar way, and brakes use friction to slow a wheel down. Friction can also cause problems. It not only makes things harder to move, but moving parts rubbing against each other wear away and become damaged. Rubbing produces heat and wastes energy. Friction can be reduced by putting a layer of oil between moving parts or by using rollers such as ball bearings to separate the parts.

National Curriculum:

Attainment Target 4: Physical Processes

At Key Stage 2 children should be taught:

> *about friction, including air resistance, as a force that slows moving things.*

At Level 3 children are expected to be able to link cause and effect in simple explanations of physical phenomena, for example the speed of an object slowing down because of the force of friction. At Level 4 children are expected to understand how motion is affected by forces of friction.

Activity:

The first activity looks at how the brakes of a bike work – when the rubber blocks of the brakes come in contact with the wheel they slow the wheel by rubbing against it. Children could look closely at their own bikes if they have them, to see the brakes working – lift the front wheel off the ground and spin it, then apply the brake. In the second activity children try to push a book along a table – friction between the book and the table will attempt to stop the book from moving. If you put more books on top of the first it will increase the friction and make the task even more difficult. Using the pencils as rollers (bearings) will make it much easier because the amount of friction has been reduced. The third activity asks children to work out different ways of using friction to stop a toy car after it has run down a slope. In the fourth activity, children try measuring friction and explore ways in which friction can be reduced. Rubbing soap on the surface, talcum powder, washing-up liquid and oil should reduce friction. The final activity on the 'Now try these' page looks at air resistance. Air resists objects as they fall – the larger the surface area of the object the greater the resistance. By gathering air in its canopy, a parachute increases air resistance and slows down a jumper's fall. Aeroplanes and cars are streamlined to help air flow over their surfaces and cut down resistance.

Teaching points:

There is less friction between slippery surfaces and more friction between rough surfaces. Look for things around the home that use friction (the bottom of track shoes, the handles of bats and rackets) or reduce friction (a squeaky door is caused by parts rubbing together – oil reduces the friction and stops the squeak).

You can easily show that friction causes heat by getting your child to rub his or her hands together – they should soon start to feel warmer.

Friction

Friction is a type of force that stops things sliding.

1 ————————————

When the brakes of a bike are put on, the bike stops.
It is **friction** that does this. As the brake pads meet, the
wheel of the bike slows down. Friction stops the wheel
turning so easily.

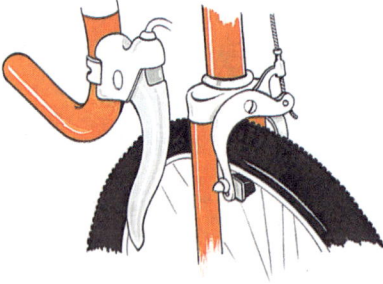

Look at these pictures. How is friction being used?

....

....

Can you think of things around the house that use friction to work?

2 ————————————

You can reduce friction.

Try and push a book along a smooth surface.

Is it easy or hard?

Now put some pencils under the book.
Does the book move more easily now?

Do you know why? ....

....

3

Try this friction test.

Make a slope as shown below. Place a toy car at the top. How can you stop the car at the bottom? Test the car out on different materials. You could try:

wood   grass   concrete   sand   carpet   lino

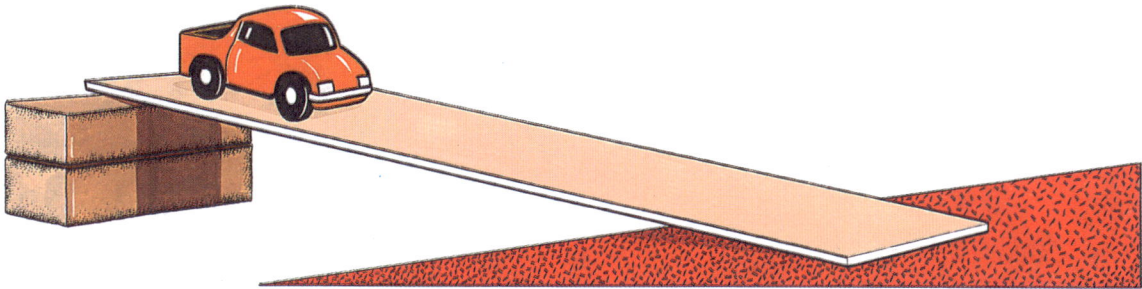

a Which one stops the car best? ....

b On which one does the car travel furthest? ....

c Do you know why? ....

....

4

You can try measuring friction.

You will need:

a block of wood
some string or cord
a clean pot
some weights

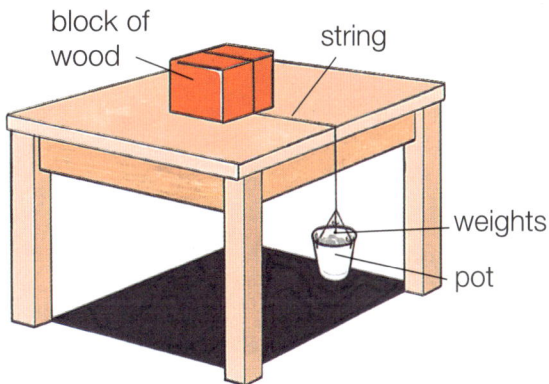

block of wood   string   weights   pot

⚠ ADULT HELP NEEDED

Hook up the pot to the string and attach the block as shown. Let the pot dangle over the table. Add weights to the pot one at a time.

What weight do you have to add to get the wood to move?

....

How could you reduce the friction between the wood and the table?

....

Now turn over ➤

Now try these ...

Air resistance slows falling or moving objects.
Parachutes use air resistance to slow the fall of a jumper.
The air inside parachutes slows down the jumper's fall.

Make your own parachute

You will need:

a newspaper
a cotton handkerchief
a plastic bag
some string
a lump of Plasticine

Make a parachute as shown. Make several parachutes in different sizes using the suggested materials.

Now drop a ball of Plasticine from a height. How long does it take to fall?

Now attach the Plasticine ball to each parachute.

Drop each one from the same height.

Which one falls the slowest?

handkerchief

string

plasticine

ADULT HELP NEEDED

....

Do you know why? ....

....

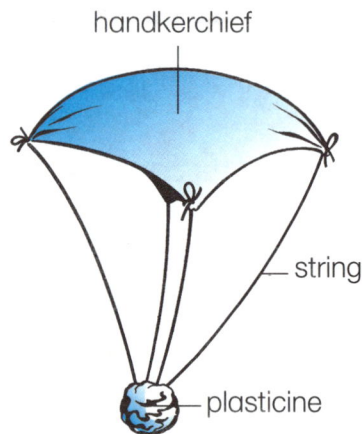

More ways to help your child:

Discuss how friction is reduced by smooth surfaces, for example sledges, an icy slope, water on a bathroom floor, the smooth surfaces of power boats and cars.

Ask your child to undo the screw top of a bottle or jar with wet or greasy hands. Now try the same thing with dry hands or with rubber gloves on.

Have a friction race. Arrange a selection of objects in a line along a smooth wooden board (include an ice-cube, a rubber and a toy car) and gradually lift up one end. Which object moves first? The objects that move more easily do so because there is less friction between their outer surface (which is smooth) and the surface of the board.

Living together

Introduction:

Animals and plants depend on each other. Plants provide food and shelter for animals. Animals help plants to make and spread their seeds and recycle nutrients back into the soil. All living things have certain needs. These include water, somewhere to live and the right food to survive. Plants and animals have adapted to survive in their environment. For example, polar bears have thick fur coats and a layer of fat under their skin to help them survive in the icy cold of the Arctic. Cacti can store water in their stems, helping them to survive long periods without rain in the desert.

National Curriculum:

Attainment Target 2: Life Processes and Living Things

At Key Stage 2 children learn about living things in their environment and are taught that:

different plants and animals are found in different habitats.

At Level 3 children should be able to identify ways in which an animal is suited to its environment, for example a fish having fins to help it swim.

Activity:

In the first activity children are asked to look at a specific habitat and select the creatures and plants that might live there. It is a good idea to talk about why these creatures and plants are suited to this particular place. In the second activity children are asked to investigate a tree. A field guide, plastic containers, an old spoon or fork, a magnifying glass and binoculars (if available) will help them in their studies. If you do not have a garden with trees, try finding a suitable park or common. The third activity provides instructions for making a study tank where children can look at a type of creature in more detail – in this case woodlice. A plastic fish tank would make an ideal study unit. Woodlice can be found under rotting logs or somewhere dark and damp. Children could carry out some simple observations to find out more about the creatures, such as trying out different types of food. In this way children will build up a fuller picture of the creature and its environment. Some woodlice curl up when touched but others do not.

A follow-up activity on the 'Now try these' page asks children to give reasons why six very different creatures are adapted to their surroundings. The list of creatures could be extended or children may come up with further ideas of their own. The last activity asks children to spot the odd creature. Again, you could make up more questions for children to try.

Teaching points:

Encourage your child's interest in small creatures that can be easily found.

Children should wear gloves when handling soil or picking up creatures. Creatures should be picked up very carefully and returned to where they were found as quickly as possible.

Living together

Animals and plants depend on each other to survive.

1

Many animals and plants can be found in a wood.

Tick the plants and animals which live in a wood.

moss	☐	**seal**	☐	**whale**	☐
fern	☐	**eagle**	☐	**lion**	☐
poppy	☐	**cactus**	☐	**owl**	☐
bluebell	☐	**beetle**	☐	**oak tree**	☐
seaweed	☐	**seagull**	☐	**spider**	☐

2

Be a tree detective

Investigate a tree near you and record what kind of plants and animals you can find. You could:

- Look carefully for signs of feeding – nibbled leaves and bark or half-eaten nuts and fruit.

- Look closely at any dead bark for insects, moss and fungi.

- Find out what lives in the leaves. Spread a large white sheet on the ground under a low leafy branch. Give the branch a quick shake. Sweep any insects or other animals that fall into collecting pots before they can scurry away. Can you identify what you have caught?

3 _____

Make your own woodlouse study tank

You will need:

a large plastic tank
some soil, rotting wood, branches, moss,
  dead leaves and stones
a plastic cover

Make up your study tank as shown. Put in
a number of woodlice. Keep the soil damp
and keep the tank somewhere shady. Feed
your woodlice with some pieces of apple,
potato or lettuce. Record what they eat and
where they like to live.

Return the woodlice to their own habitat
after two weeks.

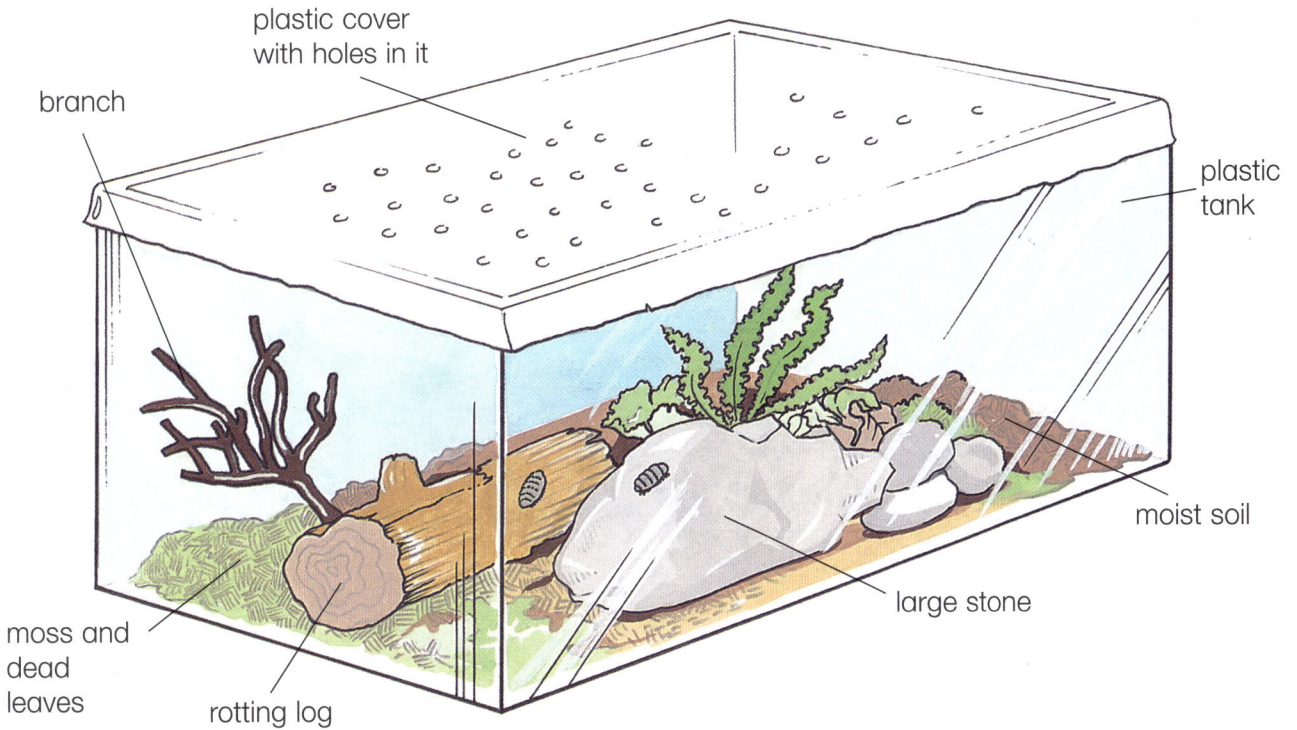

plastic cover with holes in it
branch
plastic tank
moist soil
large stone
moss and dead leaves
rotting log

Use your study tank to answer these questions.

a Do woodlice like wet or dry places?

b Do they like dark or light places?

....

....

c What happens if you touch a woodlouse?

....

Now turn over ➤

Now try these ...

1   How are these creatures adapted to their environments?

a ....

b ....

c ....

....

....

....

d ....

e ....

f ....

....

....

....

2   Which creature in each set is the odd one out? Cross it through.

a

cow   dog   frog

c

trout   eagle   swan

b

snake   bird   lizard

d

spider   fly   bee

More ways to help your child:

Make a wormery. Fill a plastic jar with alternate layers of moist soil and sand. Put one or two worms on top and cover with damp leaves. Wrap the wormery with black paper to keep out the light. What happens after a few days?

Look at birds and their beaks – birds of prey have hooked bills for tearing flesh, a hummingbird has a long bill to reach into a flower, sparrows have stubby bills to crush seeds, pelicans scoop up fish with their bills.

Discuss how animals use camouflage, for example chameleons can change colour to match their background, or a jaguar's spots hide it in the dappled light of the forest floor.

Mixing and separating

Introduction:

A solution is a liquid mixture. It forms when a substance, called a **solute**, dissolves in a liquid, called a **solvent**. A substance that dissolves is soluble. Substances that do not dissolve are insoluble. Solutions are see-through and the solute does not settle if left to stand. (In a suspension the substance clouds the liquid and eventually settles on the bottom of the container.) When a solution forms the solute spreads throughout the liquid until the solvent can dissolve no more. Many familiar liquids are solutions including syrup, vinegar, lemonade and coloured ink.

A sieve can be used to separate a solid from a liquid. Fine sieves can separate larger particles from smaller ones by trapping them in the sieve while the smaller pieces pass through. Familiar sieves include colanders and tea strainers. Filter paper is a very fine sieve: a solution would pass through, but a suspension would leave the solid in the filter.

National Curriculum:

Attainment Target 3: Materials and their Properties

At Key Stage 2 children are taught that:

mixing materials can cause them to change;
and that solid particles of different sizes can be separated by sieving.

At Level 3 children are expected to recognise that some materials can be changed and to describe those changes. At Level 4 children are expected to be able to describe some methods, such as filtration, that are used to separate simple mixtures.

Activity:

The first activity asks children to look at sugar dissolving in a cup of tea. This leads on to testing out different materials to see if they will dissolve in the second activity. After each material has been tested, the beaker should be washed out, dried and filled with water ready for the next test. The third activity asks children to see what happens when salt is added to cold and then hot water, and to compare the results. Discuss with your child beforehand how they can make sure that this test is fair (for example, use the same amount of salt and water, stir them the same number of times, use the same container). The fourth activity asks children to see how much of four different substances can be dissolved in the same amount of water. The activities on the 'Now try these' page look at separating mixtures using a sieve. If mixing up sand and stones is difficult for you to organise, then use a mixture of flour and raisins instead.

Teaching points:

Give your child the opportunity to record what happens. This can done in a notebook. Your child can then go back to it if there are any problems later.

When measuring out the different materials, make sure your child uses a level teaspoon each time otherwise the test will not be fair. Conducting fair tests is an important part of the learning process. If there is any doubt in your child's mind about the results then he or she should check their observations and repeat the experiment.

Mixing and separating

How much do you know about dissolving?

1

Put two teaspoons of sugar into a cup of hot tea (without milk) and give it a stir. Look into the cup. The sugar is no longer there.

This is called **dissolving**. The sugar has dissolved in the water. It has disappeared but it hasn't gone away. Tasting the tea will tell you that it is still there.

⚠️ ADULT HELP NEEDED

2

Some substances will dissolve and others will not.

Try dissolving one teaspoon of each of these substances in a cup of warm water from the tap.
Tick the ones that dissolve.

sand	☐	flour	☐
sugar	☐	oil	☐
salt	☐	chalk	☐
gravel	☐	washing-up liquid	☐

What happens to the substances that don't dissolve?

....

Try dissolving a sugar lump in a cup of warm water.

Now try dissolving a crushed sugar lump in warm water.

Which one dissolves faster? ....

Try stirring the water or using warmer water.

Does it make a difference? How?..

28

3

Put a teaspoon of salt into a cup of cold water and give it a stir.

Does it dissolve quickly or slowly? ....

Now put a teaspoon of salt into a cup of hot water. Give it a stir.

Does it dissolve more quickly or slowly than before?

....

Why do you think this is?

....

ADULT HELP
NEEDED

4

An amount of water can only dissolve a certain amount of a substance. After that no more will dissolve.

How many teaspoons of each of these substances will dissolve in a cup of water? Remember to use the same amount of water each time.

substance	number of teaspoons
sugar	
salt	
washing powder	
bicarbonate of soda	

Does the same amount of each substance dissolve in the water?

....

Which one dissolved the most? ....

Now turn over ➤

Now try these ...

1   Sieves are used to separate things.
Find an old sieve. Mix up some sand and stones.
Put them into the sieve and give it a shake.

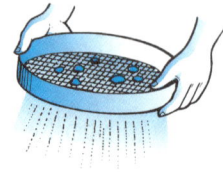

  a What happens to the stones?

  ....

  b How can a sieve be used at home?

  ....

2   Tick which of these mixtures can be separated using a sieve.

sand and gravel   salt and dried peas

flour and raisins   water and sugar

3   Take a spadeful of soil and pass it through the sieve.

  a What is left in the sieve?

  ....

  b Do you know why?

  ....

More ways to help your child:

Solutions can be separated by evaporation. Pour a solution Tof salt and water, or sugar and water,
onto a saucer. Leave it on a sunny windowsill. What happens after a few hours or a day?

Try using coffee filter papers and a cut-down lemonade bottle to make a filter. What mixtures
can your child separate with this? Try sand and water, chalk and water, and flour and water.

Switch on

Introduction:

Electricity must have a complete path to pass through a circuit – if there is a break in the circuit the current cannot flow. The idea of introducing a switch is so that you can control this flow. Switches can be used to control a variety of devices including buzzers and lights. Some devices have special automatic cut-out switches. These can be found in kettles and hair-dryers and are there to stop the appliance overheating.

Materials which let electricity flow through them are called **conductors**. Materials which do not let electricity flow through them are called **insulators**. Conductors include water, copper and silver. Electricity can also pass through the human body. People who work with electricity often wear footwear made of rubber, an excellent insulator, to protect them from being killed by an electric shock. Other materials which will not allow electricity to flow through them include wood, plastic and glass.

National Curriculum:

Attainment Target 4: Physical Processes

Children at Key Stage 2 are taught that:

a complete circuit is needed to make an electrical device work.

This work is also relevant to work done on 'Materials and their Properties' where children look at how some materials are better electrical conductors than others. At Level 3 children are expected to offer simple explanations linking cause and effect, for example a bulb failing to light when there is a break in the circuit. At Level 4 children are expected to be able to describe how a particular device in an electrical circuit can be switched on and off.

Activity:

The first activity asks children to explain what will happen when a switch is turned on. Look at the circuit with your child and discuss how it is set up before he or she attempts an answer to this question. The second activity gives simple instructions on how to make two different types of switch. The first uses two drawing pins and the switch works when the paper clip bridges the gap between the two pins. The second switch works when the two pieces of foil come together. It is a useful device for making a simple burglar alarm (place under the carpet near a door – when someone comes in they step on the switch making a light or buzzer come on). The third activity looks at which materials make good conductors of electricity. Children will probably want to try out a variety of other materials. The activities on the 'Now try these' page look at more ways to use switches and include simple instructions for testing liquids to see if they conduct electricity. When trying this out, the nails should be suspended in the liquid and not touching, otherwise they will complete the circuit on their own.

Teaching points:

Make sure that your child only uses ordinary batteries and that he or she is aware of the dangers of playing with mains electricity.

When the switches are constructed check that the connections are secure otherwise the switch may not work properly.

Switch on

Electricity needs a path or circuit to flow along.

1

Look at this circuit.

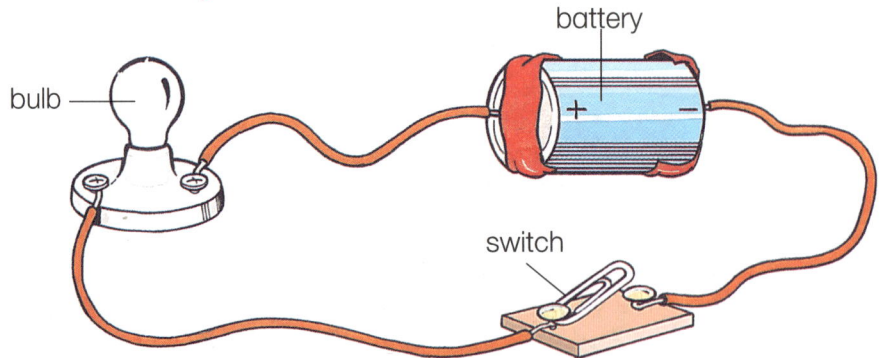

bulb

battery

switch

What will happen when the switch is pressed down?

....

Switches are very useful. They can make lights flash and control buzzers.

2

You can make your own switches.

Paper clip switch

You will need:

two drawing pins
a piece of wood
a metal paper clip

Connect up the switch as shown.

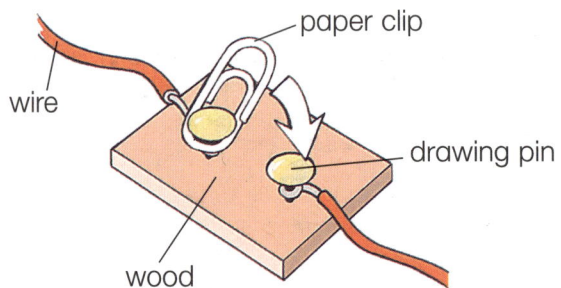

paper clip

wire

drawing pin

wood

Silver foil switch

You will need:

a piece of card about 5cm by 2cm
sticky tape
silver foil

wire   folded card   foil

sticky tape

Fold the card in two. Put a strip of foil round each end
and secure with sticky tape.
Attach your switches to a circuit. Can you explain how they work?

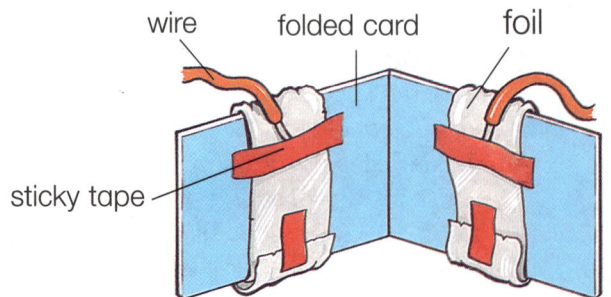

....

3

Materials which let electricity flow through them are called **conductors.**
Materials which do not let electricity flow are called **insulators**.

Test which of these materials are conductors and which are insulators.

You will need:

a battery
a torch bulb and bulb
  holder
three wires
crocodile clips
sticky tape

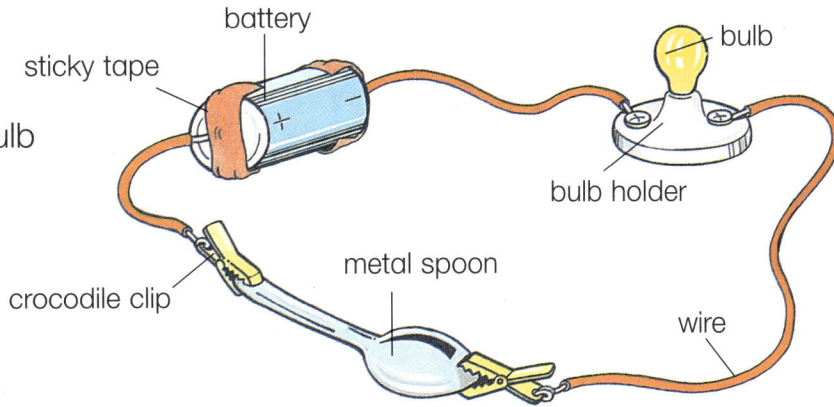

Make a circuit with the bulb and battery as shown. Connect the objects to the circuit. If the bulb lights up electricity is passing through the material.

Tick the correct box.

a metal spoon   conductor ☐   insulator ☐

b plastic pen top   conductor ☐   insulator ☐

c rubber   conductor ☐   insulator ☐

d kitchen foil   conductor ☐   insulator ☐

e cotton handkerchief   conductor ☐   insulator ☐

f pencil   conductor ☐   insulator ☐

Try testing some more objects of your own.

Now turn over ➤

Now try these ...

1   Try connecting a buzzer to a circuit with a switch.

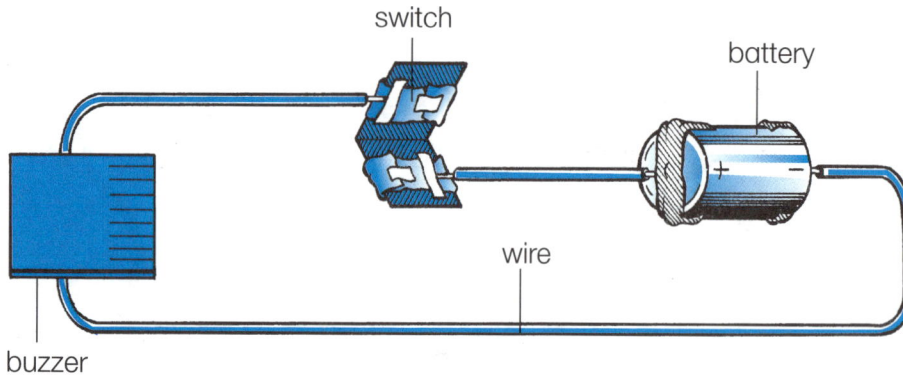

Where do you think this might be useful?

....

2   Try testing liquids to see if they conduct electricity.

You will need:

a battery
a switch
two nails
a jam jar
some card
a bulb and bulb holder
four wires
sticky tape

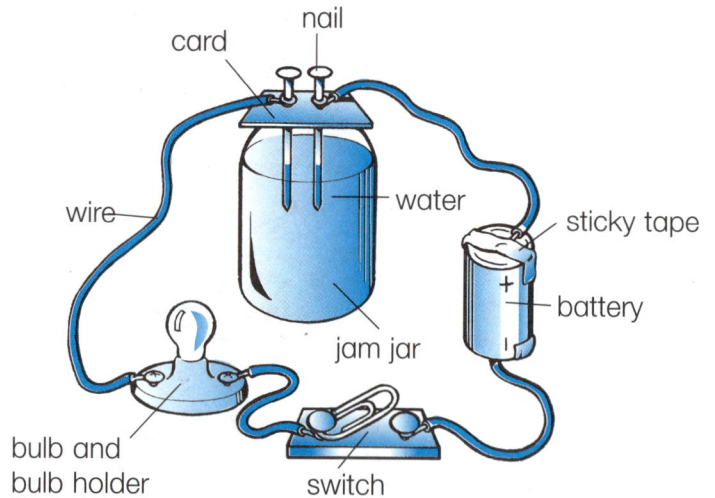

Connect up the circuit as shown. Use it to test water, lemon juice and vinegar.

More ways to help your child:

Discuss ways in which electrical insulators might be used, for example the plastic coating on the wires of an electrical appliance.

What is it?

Introduction:

Children need to understand why some materials are more suitable than others for certain jobs. The home provides a wide range of possible areas for discussion, such as talking about the different materials used to make a chair, for example wood, nails, sponge, fabric.

Materials can be split up into natural and manufactured types. Many of the things we use every day are made from natural materials, but often we are not aware of this because they have gone through several processes.

National Curriculum:

Attainment Target 3: Materials and their Properties

At Key Stage 2 children are taught to:

compare everyday materials on the basis of their properties
and to relate these properties to everyday uses of the materials.

At Level 3 children are expected to be able explain why some materials are particularly suited for specific purposes.

Activity:

All of the activities centre around the materials used in a car. The first activity asks children to name the different materials that are used in specific parts of the car. These can vary, so be ready for alternatives. The second activity asks children to explain why certain materials are used for particular jobs and to identify the properties that make them suitable. The third activity asks children to decide which materials might be used in the construction of a car. The activity then goes on to ask them why some of these materials are used. The final activities in the 'Now try these' page look at whether some materials are natural or manufactured.

Teaching points:

Get your child to talk about the materials and discuss why they might be used. Questions you can ask include: Do they break easily? Will they bend? Are they see-through? Are they good electrical conductors?

What is it?

Many of the things we use are made from different materials.

1 _____

Look at the car and write down the names of the different materials used. Use words from the list below.

plastic	rubber
glass	fabric
metal	foam

The dashboard is made from

....

The window is made from

....

The body is made from

....

The tyres are made from

....

The number plate is made from

....

2

Why is it a good idea:

a to make the windscreen from glass?

....

....

b to make the body of the car out of metal?

....

....

c to use plastic and fabric inside the car?

....

....

seats are made from

....

3

a Tick the materials below which would be useful when building a car.

wood	☐	gold	☐
iron	☐	water	☐
steel	☐	rubber	☐
plastic	☐	aluminium	☐
oil	☐	paint	☐

b Which liquid is found in the radiator of a car?

....

c Why do the tyres of a car need to last a long time?

....

....

The headlamp is made from

....

Now turn over ➤

Now try these ...

1   What materials can be used to make these things?

cup   ....      glove   ....

ruler   ....      key   ....

shoe   ....      soft toy   ....

2   Are any of the things made from natural materials? Which ones?

....

Are any of them made from more than one material? Which ones?

....

3   Some materials may have to go through many stages to make things.
Fill in the spaces in these chains.

wheat   →   [ ]   →   bread

clay   →   [ ]   →   wall

wood   →   [ ]   →   books

More ways to help your child:

Discuss with your child what oil is used for in a car. How is water used?

Look for items around your home that are made from more than one material. Why do different materials have to be used? For example, a saucepan may be made of metal but the handle is made of plastic. The metal conducts heat well and the plastic protects your hand because it doesn't conduct heat.

Good vibrations

Introduction:

Musical sounds can be produced in a number of different ways. In a violin the sounds are made by plucking or passing a bow across the string. A wind instrument such as a clarinet has a reed that vibrates and makes a column of air inside the instrument vibrate as well. Holes are covered and uncovered to change the length of the column of air. We are most used to sound waves travelling through air, however, sound can travel through water, metal or any other material.

Sound proofing is very important today. Double glazing is used in houses and other forms of sound insulation are used in recording studios and elsewhere. People who are exposed to high levels of sound usually wear ear protectors.

National Curriculum:

Attainment Target 4: Physical Processes

At Key Stage 2 children are taught that:

*the pitch and loudness of sounds can be changed; and that
vibrations from sound sources can travel through a variety of materials.*

At Level 3 children should be able to link cause and effect, for example the tightening of a string makes the note higher. At Level 4 they should be able to explain that sounds are heard through a variety of materials.

Activity:

In the first activity, children are asked to make a simple stringed instrument. If you are unable to find any balsa wood to make the instrument then use two pencils instead. The activity goes on to use the instrument to look at ways of altering the pitch of the note. Three things affect pitch: the tension of the string, its thickness and length. Children are encouraged to alter the tension and thickness of the string, but you could reduce or increase the length of the string by moving the balsa wood bridges or pressing on the string half-way along its length. The second activity experiments with sound travelling through different materials. Sound travels faster through denser materials than it does through air. For example, sound travels faster and further through water than through air. The third activity looks at how loud sounds are (measured in decibels) and the activities on the 'Now try these' page examine how sound proofing works.

Teaching points:

The pitch of a note is how high or how low a note sounds. Fast vibrations create high notes, while slow vibrations create low ones.

To make a very simple wind instrument, your child could try putting a blade of grass between his or her fingers and using it as a reed.

Most sound proofing materials tend to be soft so that they can absorb the different pressure changes caused by vibration. Get your child to see how much sound is cut out when they have the hood of their coat up or when they are wearing headphones.

Good vibrations

How can you change the sound of a note?

1

When you stretch a string tighter you can make a higher note.
On a guitar or violin the strings are stretched to make different notes.

ADULT HELP NEEDED

Make a simple stringed instrument

You will need:

a piece of wood
some balsa wood
a nail
some nylon fishing line
some marbles
a clean yoghurt pot

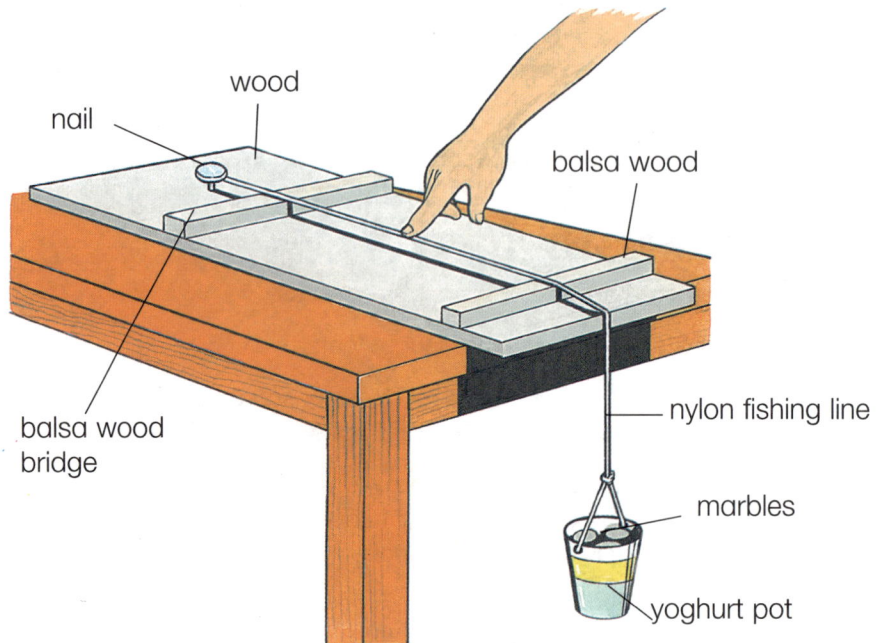

Bang the nail into the wood.
Attach one end of the fishing line to the nail.
Fit two pieces of balsa wood under the line.
Fix a pot to the end of the line.
Put some marbles in the pot so that the string is really tight.
Try plucking or scraping the string.

a What happens when you pluck the string?

....

b What happens if you add extra weights to the pot?

....

c Try using different thicknesses of string. Does the thicker string change the sound of the note? How?

....

2

Sound can travel through many different materials. It can travel through air, water and solid objects.

Place a watch at one end of a wooden table. Can you hear it at the other end?

Try listening to the watch through these materials:

carpet

concrete

cardboard

glass

water (fill a balloon with water and put the watch on the other side)

Which material can you hear through best? ....

3

How loud is a sound? Sound is measured in **decibels**.

Put these sounds in order, starting with the quietest. Number them from 1 to 5.

passing aircraft		150 decibels	☐
leaves rustling		10 decibels	☐
stereo playing		50 decibels	☐
people whispering		20 decibels	☐
busy city street		90 decibels	☐

Now turn over ➤

Now try these ...

It is possible to keep sounds out by using **sound proofing**.

Put an alarm clock into a shoe box.
Fill the box with newspaper. Put the lid on top.

alarm clock

newspaper

shoe box

Does the clock's tick sound louder or quieter?

Now try filling the box with these materials. Which is the best material for sound proofing? Tick the correct boxes.

cardboard	good ☐	bad ☐
polystyrene	good ☐	bad ☐
cotton	good ☐	bad ☐
wool	good ☐	bad ☐
egg boxes	good ☐	bad ☐
wood	good ☐	bad ☐

More ways to help your child:

Encourage your child to try other sound proofing materials.

Discuss with your child other ways of keeping noise and sound out, for example double glazing. Make some headphones from wire, card and sponge or other material.

Talk to your child about echoes and how these are produced. Discuss why lightning is seen before thunder is heard. Talk about how bats use echo-location to find food.

It's a fair test

Introduction:

Scientific investigation is a core part of science in the National Curriculum. While there are no facts to be learnt, the ability to carry out systematic investigations, record results and draw conclusions is important throughout children's science work. It requires a variety of skills and practices that need to be encouraged. Asking questions is a vital part of any science activity and being able to predict, record and interpret results will help with further science work. Children should be encouraged to use a systematic approach to science, interpreting their results, recording them accurately and drawing conclusions from their findings.

National Curriculum:

Attainment Target 1: Experimental and Investigative Science

At Key Stage 2 children are taught to:

*turn ideas suggested to them, and their own ideas,
into a form that can be investigated;
make careful observations and measurements;
use tables, bar charts and line graphs to present results; and
to use results to draw conclusions.*

At Level 3 children should be able to carry out a fair test, explaining why it is fair. They should record their observations in a variety of ways and say what they have found out from their work. At Level 4 children should present their observations using tables, bar charts and simple graphs and interpret patterns or trends in their data.

Activity:

The first activity requires children to consider whether or not the testing that has taken place is fair. They are then asked to examine some of the results taken from the test and then use these results to answer questions and draw conclusions. Children should be encouraged to carry out a similar test and think up some more questions to ask. The activities on the 'Now try these' page also look at whether a test is fair or not.

Teaching points:

It is important to discuss with your child the reason for a fair test. Encourage your child to consider the way a test has been organised before it is set up, so that the results will be accurate.

If your child decides to try out the test, collect together a number of balls of the same size. Each ball should be dropped (not thrown) from the same height and onto the same surface. Your child may suggest other tests that he or she would like to try out.

It's a fair test

Do you know how to carry out a fair test?

1 _____

Charlotte, Joe, Zoe and Bradley have been asked to find out
how high four different balls will bounce. They use a rubber ball,
a tennis ball, a golf ball, and a hollow plastic ball.
They each have a go at carrying out the test.

Charlotte drops the balls from different heights onto carpet, lino,
concrete and grass.

Joe drops the balls from the same height onto carpet, lino,
concrete and grass.

Zoe and Bradley drop all the balls from the same height
onto the same surface – concrete.

a Who carried out the fairest test?

....

b Why were the other tests unfair?

....

....

2

Here are the results of the fairest test.
The balls were dropped on concrete from a
height of 80 centimetres.

type of ball	height it bounced
golf ball	52cm
hollow plastic ball	26cm
tennis ball	48cm
rubber ball	35cm

a Which ball bounced the highest? ....

b Which ball bounced the lowest? ....

c Why did some balls bounce higher than others?

    ....

    ....

d Would the type of surface make any difference to the height
   the balls bounced?

    ....

    ....

3

Try out the test above for yourself. Make sure it is as fair as possible.

Make up some of your own questions.

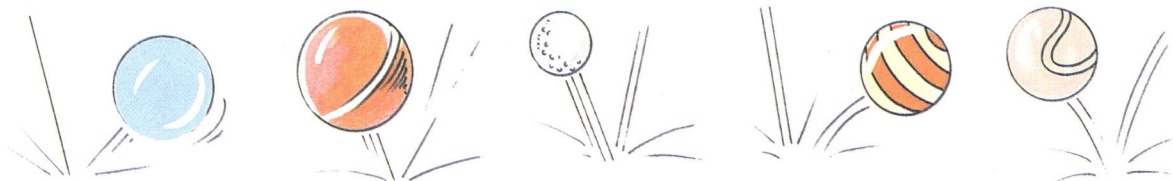

Now turn over ➤

Now try these ...

It is important that you always make sure that any experiment is a fair test.

How could you make sure that these are fair tests?

1

How far a toy car travels on different surfaces.

....

....

....

2

Measuring the temperature each day.

....

....

....

3

Measuring to see how much a plant has grown in a week.

....

....

....

4

Dissolving different substances in some water.

....

....

....

More ways to help your child:

Get your child to keep a record of his or her tests and experiments in a notebook. This will be useful if anything needs to be checked or if your child has to look back at the results.

ANSWERS

In some cases, the answers given here are examples only. It may well be that your child will come up with other suggestions which are acceptable.

pages 4–5

1 The plant that grows best should be one in a warm, sunny spot. Plants will grow in the dark, but they will look yellow and weak.

2 The roots should start to grow down into the water.

3 The inside of the bag should be covered in water droplets. The water is given off by the leaves.

4 The shoot is searching for the light so that its leaves can start to make food.

page 6

1 It goes yellow because there is no sunlight. Plants need sunlight to go green.

pages 8–9

1 transparent: glass, oil
translucent: plastic, tissue paper, milk
opaque: thick curtain, silver foil, mirror, leather.

2 a The shadow gets bigger.
  b The shadow gets smaller.
  c The closer the cut-out is to the torch, the more light it stops from reaching the wall.

3 good reflectors: silver, bronze, steel, water, polished wood.

4 back: you can see a lot more of the room behind you, the image is the right way up.
front: the image looks bigger and is upside-down.

pages 10

The light beams change direction.
The light beams are scattered by the silver foil, especially if it has been scrunched up.

pages 12–13

1 Springs are used in chairs, on doors and gates, in ballpoint pens, etc.

2 The spring should be drawn more tightly coiled.
The spring is squashed/becomes shorter.

3 The elastic band is stretched. It springs back when the weight is taken out of the pot.

page 14

If the boat was going forwards it will now go backwards and vice versa.

pages 16–17

1

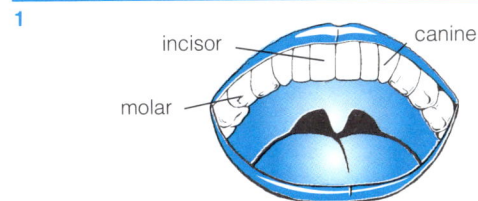

incisor · canine · molar

2 toothpaste, toothbrush, floss, water
clean your teeth after meals.
3 carrot, milk, water, apple
4 The shell should be gradually eaten away.

page 18

1 decay   incisor
  canine   molar
  milk   gum
  dentist   toothpaste

2

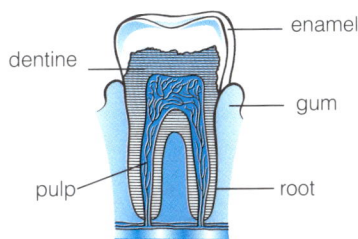

enamel · dentine · gum · pulp · root

pages 20–21

1 Friction helps the woman's shoes grip the ground so that she can push the car.
Friction between the tyre and the road stops the car spinning off.

2 The pencils reduce the friction between the book and the table.

3 Of the examples given, sand should stop the car best and it will travel furthest on lino.

4 You could reduce friction by using oil, grease, water, talcum powder etc.

page 22

The parachute with the largest canopy should fall the slowest because it catches most air.

pages 24–25

1 moss, fern, bluebell, beetle, owl, oak tree, spider

3 Woodlice like wet and dark places best. Some woodlice curl up if you touch them.

page 26

1 for example:
  a A polar bear has thick fur to protect it against the cold.
  b A dolphin's streamlined shape helps it cut through the water.
  c A frog has large webbed feet for swimming.
  d A woodpecker has a long, sharp beak for tapping into the trunk to look for insects.
  e A giraffe's long neck helps it reach high branches.
  f A camel's humps store food.

2 a frog
  b bird
  c trout
  d spider

pages 28–29

2 sugar, salt, washing-up liquid
Those that don't dissolve sink or float on the water.
The crushed sugar lump will dissolve faster.
Stirring and using warmer water will make the sugar dissolve faster.

3 a It should dissolve slowly in cold water.
  b It should dissolve more quickly in warm water.
  c Heat helps things to dissolve more easily.

page 30

1 a They get left behind in the sieve.
  b Sieves are used at home to sieve flour; to separate vegetables from cooking water; to strain tea leaves.

2 All the mixtures can separate except water and sugar.

3 Stones and large lumps are left in the sieve.
Soil is small enough to pass through a sieve but the stones and large lumps of soil are not.

pages 32–33

1   The light will go on.

2   Switches work by completing the circuit which lets the electricity flow.

3   **a** conductor
    b insulator
    c insulator
    d conductor
    e insulator
    f wood – insulator
        pencil lead – conductor

page 34

2   As an alarm or a door bell.

pages 36–37

1   for example:
    seats: fabric and foam
    headlamps: plastic
    window: glass
    body: metal
    tyres: rubber
    number plate: plastic
    dashboard: plastic

2   **a** Because you can see through it.
    b Because it will last a long time and protect you.
    c Because it is easy to shape and comfortable to sit on.

3   **a** steel, plastic, oil, rubber, aluminium, paint
    b water
    c Because they are constantly being worn away as they rub against the road.

page 38

3   flour
    bricks
    paper

pages 40–41

1   **a** The string vibrates and makes sound.
    b The note should get higher.
    c The thicker the string the lower the note.

3   passing aircraft   5

    leaves rustling   1

    stereo playing   3

    people whispering   2

    busy city street   4

pages 44–45

1   **a** Zoe and Bradley.
    b Because the others did not drop the balls from the same height onto the same surface.

2   **a** golf ball
    b hollow plastic ball
    c because they were made from different materials
    d Yes, because balls bounce better on hard, smooth surfaces.

page 46

1   Make sure that the car always starts at the same spot. Do not change the angle of the slope.

2   Take the temperature at the same time and same place each day.

3   Always measure the plant starting at the same point.

4   Use the same amount of each substance. Use the same amount of water at the same temperature.